HOW TO ACTIVATE A WINNER'S MINDSET

SHARAYAH WALKER

SHAY ON A MISSION

WWW.SELFPUBLISHN30DAYS.COM

Published by *Self Publish -N- 30 Days*

Printed in the United States of America

ISBN: 979-8-82196-533-2

1. Nonfiction 2. Self-Help 3. General

Sharayah "Shay on a Mission" Walker, *Mental Muscle: How to Activate a Winner's Mindset*

Disclaimer/Warning:

This book is intended for lecture and informative purposes only. This publication is designed to provide competent and reliable information regarding the subject matter covered. The author or publisher are not engaged in rendering legal or professional advice. Laws vary from state to state and if legal, financial, or other expert assistance is needed, the services of a professional should be sought. The author and publisher disclaim any liability that is incurred from the use or application of the contents of this book.

This book was created for those holding themselves back. I challenge you all to start building your mental muscle to live the life you desire.

Table of Contents

Introduction

Having mental muscle is about mindset training to build stamina, which allows you to overcome challenges that distract or derail you off course in life. It takes time, experience, and perseverance to build a mindset where you're not playing the victim, but becoming the overcomer. It's about gaining the confidence to not just stay in your comfort zone, but to do the unknown with resiliency and fight for a mission bigger than yourself.

Over the years, I have taken my life more seriously by studying and modeling the successes of Grant Cardone, Elena Cardone, Oprah, Tyler Perry, Steve Harvey, Evan Carimicheal, Eric Thomas, and Daymond John, to name a few.

By modeling the success of such greats, it has allowed me to create the mental stamina to handle adversities. This led me to correct my mindset, check my emotions, become a better decision maker, and even watch the company I keep. Each person above has gifted me the will to write this book and to empower others to believe that they can do anything they put their mind to.

I know, it's a cliché, right? You have probably heard this hundreds, if not thousands, of times. But you need to continuously hear it.

Zig Ziglar stated it best: "Repetition is the mother of learning and the father of action, which makes it the architect of accomplishment." So, let me say it again, you can do it, no matter what "it" is with the right attitude.

I hope that this book empowers you to win at life. It is not always about the good times, but it's about learning to embrace the unpleasant moments as well. Life is what you make it to be, but it takes time to build that muscle so that you can overcome the inevitable and the impossible.

Still, I know you can do it. So, let's get started!

CHAPTER 1

Deal with Your Pain

"The past doesn't define you, your present does. It's okay to create a vision of the future because it affects your behavior in the 'now,' but don't dwell on past mistakes. Learn from them and focus on those lessons for the moment. That's where change can really happen."

—Jillian Michaels

Mental health is true wealth. Society (which includes you) must quit sweeping it underneath the rug! Life is ninety percent mentality. There comes a point when you have to deal with the pain hindering your growth and decide to be the judge of yourself for the better.

At that point, you become your own critic, learning to swerve through uncertainties and uncontrollable circumstances. You must end the "shoulda," "coulda," and "woulda" thoughts. When you are able to harness these thoughts, you stop screwing yourself. Instead, you flourish.

Now, I'm not saying shifting your perception is going to make everything easy. You will face adversity with losses. Everyone does. The point is to not view them as losses.

Change losses into lessons, and your tough experiences into personal development. Then, you will become the person you are destined to be. Choose now to be a victor over a victim, because life is going to move on with or without you.

But, how do we do that? First, we must find the source of our victim mentality, and that usually comes from pain. I don't believe in embracing to stay stuck, but I do believe in addressing it. Learning to address the hurt will help you acknowledge the unresolved issues from childhood, unsealed trauma, and life's other turmoils. Pain is the very thing that can hinder or inspire our progress. It molds us, but if we're not careful, it can also fold us.

I can tell you from personal experience that my unresolved childhood trauma has both hindered my growth and made me the woman I am working to be. It goes both ways, but you must stop sweeping things underneath the rug.

For example, when I told close acquaintance of mine the need of counseling at the age fifteen, that individual laughed at me. This situation wasn't even close to resolved until my late twenties, which was a lesson learned that caused me decades of time by not standing up for myself. This behavior is an avoidance of suffering will inevitably unravel into chaos as time goes by. It is vitally important to your mental health that you make it a priority so that you face your misery head-on so that you will no longer be holding yourself back from being the best version of yourself.

Being the best version of yourself will not only get you into the driving direction that you are to go but it will help identify what triggers and trends you will notice as you mature. In life, you will have setbacks, setups, and comebacks which will cause you to go through a mental health roller coaster.

Pain Avoidance

Before you can come up with a plan, you must first identify the pain you are avoiding to develop the proper mindset. I know you may be wondering what your mindset has to do with pain. It all comes down to how far you will go to create the life that you envision.

Growing up, I always heard the concept of "manning up." This could be for women and men. I gathered this meant you shouldn't show pain. Pain equals weakness (at least in my upbringing). And you don't want to be weak. Only the strong survive, right?

I am here to tell you that dealing with your pain isn't weakness. It's a tactic because it will catch up to you if you don't. Hey, remember my story. It's what I did for almost fifteen years. I suppressed my internal struggles and just kept on sweeping my pain underneath the rug year after year.

Avoiding internal battles will manifest in how you build

relationships with people, from your immediate family to your friends (my friends are considered my "framily").

I told my inner circle how when I was twenty-nine, I didn't want to live in this world anymore because everyone would be better off without me. My former relationships, especially my nine-year dead relationship, gave me the notion that I was not good enough or worthy to be loved by family, friends, or anyone. This was one of the first times in my adult life I really considered suicide. But, by the grace of my inner circle, I was able to seek the assistance I needed to resolve these thoughts and remove anything that would be hindering my growth as well as moving forward to heal.

Acknowledging this key factor in my life has been a key to positioning me into the version I am becoming. There is nothing like getting that weight off your shoulders. This will be the focal point of going in a new direction. It will bring you a world of new opportunities and a fulfilling purpose to grow into the person that God has designed you to be.

I can honestly say that once I acknowledged my mental health hindrances, I changed as a woman. My life transformed for the better. Now, I know my triggers. I still seek help, knowing that I am not in this everlasting mental health journey alone, yet, I progress forward as the woman I am destined to be.

I coach mindset practices to my clients that are aspiring entrepreneurs and speak life into my viewers, illustrating that one's mindset is the focal of their life. I even stated, as part of the five M's of entrepreneurial foundation, that mindset is like the foundation of a house. If your mindset is right, then your house will not collapse in a storm.

You cannot build a house from the roof down, so why would you think you can build a strong and enduring life without dealing with your deepest pain? When you are committed to your healing process, you want to plan what needs to be changed, execute the actionable steps on how you are going to resolve this situation and then monitor your progress. This is why I developed in this next section, how I have created a mental health priority plan based on my personal experiences to elaborate on paid avoidance.

Mental Health Priority Plan

To make mental health a priority, seek assistance. I did, and I will continually pursue the mental maintenance that puts me in the mindset to flourish. It is imperative that you create a mental health priority plan so you can accomplish the healing you desire.

I want to fully disclose that I am not a mental health specialist, so I am going by my personal experiences and the resources I used throughout my journey. If you are looking or thinking you need a mental health specialist, I recommend you include your inner circle when searching for recommendations.

You will be surprised with how many people have therapists and mental health counselors. I know I was shocked and felt that my mental health journey was not abnormal. I know a few myself that were willing to let me know they were going to counseling themselves.

You can also look online by using search engines on mental health counselors or therapy, and contact crisis service/suicide prevention support in your area to give you recommendations. In the meantime, I have created a mental health priority plan for you as you do your research and make the best decision that fits you best.

But, how do you create a mental health priority plan? Below I have provided the steps to dealing with your pain, so that you can put yourself in a great position to start your mental health journey.

Step 1: Acknowledge your problem. Accept that it's okay to not be okay, but you have to *want* to get some resolution to be at peace with your life.

Step 2: Seek help, whether it's a spiritual advisor, a therapist, or a counselor. If you don't know where to start, research mental health counselors in your area online and you will be able to screen through who you see fit as a counselor. Also, most areas have a crisis services hotline that you can research out to twenty-four-seven until you find a professional that fulfills your needs.

Step 3: Let your inner circle know what is going on, so that they can support your mental healing journey. This can be scary, but it's time to realize that you no longer want to suppress your feelings and those who support you will support you throughout this journey. Thank God for my supporting cast because I for sure would not live to see my living days without them.

Step 4: Create a village of like-minded and success-focused people that you can network with. Choose the people you decide to be around wisely. You find these network people by being open to yourself to conferences, local meetup events, support groups, national organizations. You can find these people and groups virtually and in person.

Step 5: Get a journal where you start self-discovery practices to filter out negative thoughts and things that you believe are holding you back. When a setback happens in your life, how are you feeling? Journaling is a great stress reliever to get things out of your head that hinder your growth.

Step 6: Pick someone that you trust to keep you accountable. Whether they are your counselor, therapist, or your coach, make a point to see them regularly.

Following these steps will allow you to bring out the greatness within. Tapping into your inner power that lies within you is dependent on your ability to stop avoiding the pain and to correct the problems in your life head-on, so you can progress forward instead of being held back.

This plan will be your roadmap to a winners mindset. But, in addition to having a plan, I suggest you identify what makes you avoid your pain. Why do you feel the need to sweep your feelings underneath the rug, and why it is not healthy for you to suppress your feelings?

The next chapter will discuss how your influence as your own critic will distinguish how long it takes for your greatness to be discovered. Also, as you are filling out the guided questions, be sure to take action and write your responses to my Instagram (@shayonamission).

GUIDED QUESTIONS:

1. *What is the significance of dealing with pain?*

2. *Think about the things holding you back from having a winning mindset. What are they?*

3. *What steps toward mental healing can you implement in your life right now?*

Inspiration Sources:

- *Mindset* by Carol Dweck

CHAPTER 2

You are Your Biggest Critic

"Don't limit yourself. Many people limit themselves to what they think they can do. You can go as far as your mind lets you. What you believe, remember, you can achieve."

— Mary Kay Ash

It's time to start living through your greatness, because you are destined for more. Building mental muscle will create a thick skin to protect you from critics, nemeses, support saboteurs (people who say they want to support you, but hinder your growth and laugh at your journey), and anybody else who doesn't understand your mission in life.

I started with the notion that you are your biggest critic. Before anybody judges you, you judge yourself. We all have self-sabotaged ourselves at one point or another.

I'm sure you're quite familiar with some of the below statements:

- *"I look fat in that dress."*

- *"They make everything look so easy."*
- *"I am just trying to make everyone happy."*
- *"I am just going to work for the rest of my life?"*
- *"Because it's how I was raised; I just might as well accept it."*

Through this negativity, we predetermine our outlook on life before we even get the opportunity to live and see how our future is written. I am here to tell you that being your own biggest critic is not conducive to your growth.

Let's go more in-depth with negative affirming criticism. This next section will elaborate on how your willpower to win in life will hinder your growth from negative critics. Also, the negative-affirming critics will help you evolve good or bad its your choice. The stories backed up by two great stories then after will support how to overcome the negative critic thoughts that we all have endured in one aspect of our lives.

Negative-Affirming Critic

Starting with the bad is excruciating, but I like to think that every negative situation aids in our growth as individuals. Yes, it is true that what doesn't kill you makes you stronger. The things you learn to become better from a bad situation can make you even more powerful.

Let's break down where this critical internal evaluation comes from:

- *Pain*
- *Unresolved issues*

- *Negative thought processes*
- *Poor mindsets*
- *Limited beliefs*

To really move forward and stop being so damn hard on yourself, let's get more intact with overcoming being your biggest critic by developing internal principles. Based on the knowledge that I have gathered, these are my principles to overcome critical internal evaluation:

1. Acknowledge that your feelings matter. This life and the pain you have or may experience in the future is part of your story.
2. Stop sweeping things underneath the rug—meaning, stop just letting things go with no healing. Even if you can't get closure from another party, you can still learn to accept, heal, and deal with the situation and move on.

Take my life, for example. Before my business grew where it is today, I faced countless rejections. People didn't know me, so they didn't want me to coach them. They didn't trust me. I needed to build the brand. Did I sit down and cry? Maybe a little. But, did I give up? No!

Instead, I did the following:

a. **Accept.** Accept that all people are not my ideal clients.
b. **Heal**. Heal from knowing that just because they didn't see I was good fit, I would be a good fit for somebody.
c. **Deal.** Deal with the rejection and understand that who is for me, is for me, and who is not, is not. It is best that

I continue to make changes as I see fit and keep things going. The right people will come along to sign up to my services when the time is right.

After accepting, dealing, and healing, you are still not done doing the work, which leads to keeping things built up inside you and that has got to stop to improve. Step three goes more in-depth as to what I mean by holding inside your deepest and darkest demons.

3. Stop bottling things up. Are you waiting to explode? The world is not on your shoulders. You cannot be all things for everybody. If you aren't ready to deal with what you are going through, how can you overcome it? Ignoring it is the problem. Dealing with it is the solution, which will take courage.
4. Stop going with the flow without meaning or purpose. Do you want to start to live life or are you just going to keep on existing?
5. Look inside to find what you want in life. If you don't know what you want yet, that's fine, but how do you plan to discover your dreams? What can you do daily to find yourself?
6. You don't have to be alone in this.

Remember, when you have self-doubt, trust you will never be perfect. You're human, and you shall make mistakes. You can't make everybody happy.

On the flip side, I am the type of person who believes you can always change negativity into positivity. You can learn how to become the better person you are destined to be based on the experiences that make you who you are. It's great when you analyze what you can do better the next time around.

I would like to share some stories of affirmation and positive critique that display how you can self-evaluate. Although I could have picked countless stories that have inspired over the years, I selected two great ones. The first is about my favorite basketball players, more so, how what he does off the court than on the court. This is Lebron James.

Later, I will touch on a woman who had to endure and overcome a lot of negative criticism. Now, she has a million-dollar empire, and she did it all by channeling out the negative thinking of others and refusing to internalize those thoughts that kept her from winning in life.

Lebron James, the "King James" Era

In the beginning before Lebron James was labeled the King, he was just a kid from Akron raised by a single mom and eventually got married to his high school sweetheart who were teenage parents. He could have let his dream subside as a professional athlete to being what society could have allowed him to be a dropout with being a teen father. But with all that he experienced he still pressed forward as he still progressed forward in his career. As he continued in his career, Lebron James was hated by many fans and new critics because of how he received so much press and acknowledgment when some didn't like how he played the game. Still, he was respected by many more.

Yes, Lebron James won four out of ten titles in eleven years. This was during his eighteen-year career, and it's still counting. Yet, he is constantly compared to other greats like Michael Jordan, Magic Johnson, Kobe Bryant, Larry Bird, and Bill Russell.

Nevertheless, he still had to critique himself throughout his career to be the best person he could be on and off the court. He knew he had to progress if he wanted to be declared the G.O.A.T. (greatest of all time).

He had to judge and study what he needed to do as the leader of his team to get his teammates involved to earn these championships, by watching the greats. During the NBA finals in 2014, Lebron James had to overcome the pain of a cramp in his leg. He could have turned in and said, "I quit," allowing the press to scrutinize his every move like he wasn't one of the greats like Michael Jordan(MJ) because MJ had flu-like symptoms.

With all the adversity he dealt with, he overcame negativity within himself and others and won one of the final games in the championship.

Although he didn't win the championship that year, he went on the next two years with no championships. He had to deal with more negative criticism from being a bully on the court but continued to stay focused and accept he was great. He continues to be great by starting non-profits, opening up schools in his hometown, and giving scholarships to those in need.

Eventually, back on the court, he returned home to Cleveland and won his third championship, however, afterwards, he dealt with more negative press from not having enough championships. This can bring some people to say they are never good enough. But not Lebron James. He pressed on and did get his fourth championship with the Lakers (even after he got scrutiny for making a superpower team).

The moral of this story reflects back that with all the pain Lebron James had to endure. He could have thrown in the towel a long time ago and walked away from the game, but he didn't let the negativity from within or of others hinder his growth as a man and ruin passion for basketball.

This shows how you have to deal with adversities the same way that Lebron James had to overcome. Imagine how powerful your story can be when you share how you dealt with adversity and became the greatest version of yourself.

Mary Kay Story

The most moving story I have ever heard was about Mary Kay. She broke through her own personal tragedies. Her husband returned from war only to leave her for another woman. She found herself alone, and her children fatherless.

Then, her second husband unexpectedly died when she

was just about to start her own company (during a time when it was a true "man's world," where women could only hope to take behind-the-scenes credit, and men garnered all the praise and acknowledgment for their achievements).

She was passed over for countless promotions, while they were given to male coworkers whom she helped train and did less work than she did. Sure, Mary Kay could have given herself up, saying she was never going make it, and give up.

Instead, she elevated.

Mary Kay did the complete opposite of sulking and hiding from tragedy by building a multi-million-dollar company.

She did this by not letting others tell her that should quit because she had dealt with:

- Being a widower.
- Overcoming a man's world.
- Get overpassed by countless promotions from those that she helped her male associates.

By dealing with all these adversities, she became successful in our own rite of passage by not allowing the limited thinkers or being in a man's world to hinder her from having a multi-million-dollar empire that outlived her. She became a millionaire, setting up over 3.5 million sales people worldwide. She changed the game for female business owners across the world.

As you can see, these two stories of Lebron James and Mary Kay Ash counteracts their way of thinking and how they have made an impact in this world. Don't let life just pass you by with the abnormal, unpopular thinking that you start to think "I shoulda did this with my time," "I coulda been this person if I didn't make that choice in my life," or "I woulda been this if I didn't get involved with these types of people." All these internal thoughts, we will elaborate in more depth in the next chapter.

GUIDED QUESTIONS:

1. *Make a list of five things that you frequently critique yourself on.*

2. *Where does the root cause of your pain come from?*

3. *What action steps are you gonna start taking now to get closer to the person you want to become?*

Inspiration Sources:

- *Built to Serve* by Evan Carmichael
- *Finding Love After Heartbreak* by Stephan Labossiere
- *Start with Your Why and Finding Your Why* by Simon Sinek

CHAPTER 3

Stop Living in the Shoulda, Coulda, Woulda

*"If you're not happy right now,
it's because you're not serving enough people,
or you're not serving the people in your life deeply enough."*

— Evan Carmichael

When you're living your life in the past, you're living a life of unfulfillment with no purpose or clarity! It's easy to go back in time and think, *if I had done this differently, my life could have been this way. If we had done more while this person was living, then we would have had a better relationship.*

I know we've all been there.

Personally, mine included:

- I *shoulda* changed my major in college from business to a mental health field.

- I *coulda* have had a corporate job or been impacting others as a doctor or as a counselor helping others overcome distresses and adversities.
- This action change of events *woulda* put me in a better financial position, and I probably would have been married and with kids by now.

I can go on as taking different actions would have changed my life and given me a different perspective about what is most important. The section will go into another time travel perspective. We will review how my life could have changed at birth if things had gone differently.

Time Traveling Perspective

Let me play out the time traveling scenario for you. Let's say my mother decided to stay in California instead of moving 3,000 miles to Buffalo in 1992 to reunite with my father. My life surely would have been different living in warm weather for nine months out of the year instead of only four to five. Buffalo winters can surely be brutal; the sunshine would have been great!

Who knows how my relationships would have been with my siblings, what kind of friendships I could have built, the career I could have had, or the family that I might have created? Yes, surely my life would have been a stranger to me now. I could have been married, been a mother by now. Maybe I would have been a business owner making six or seven figures, or been someone else entirely.

But, what could have been doesn't matter because it's not what is now. I am thirty-four year old and may have been born in Oakland, but my hometown will always be Buffalo. I was raised in a two-parent family with three siblings, and two others we claimed.

I don't have the best relationships with family, but I do know I have the best friends that are supplemental to being my family that I wouldn't trade for the world. I earned two degrees and am now working to elevate to being a full-time entrepreneur and philanthropist. Overall, I can honestly say that my life is as it is supposed to be.

Although a new exciting life is nice to daydream about, I see how blessed I am and don't take for granted those in my life and the path that I am on. Everything happens for a reason.

If my parents did not relocate to Buffalo, there probably would have been no Ramon, Tracy, Aungalique, Sonya, Coach T, Tim, Marcy, Gabrielle, Kenyana, Leah, Chrissy, Jennifer, Christina, Aimiamia, Yakima Chip, or Paulie. The list goes on! These are the people that have significantly impacted me.

I know there will be new people that I will be exposed to more as time goes by. People meet you at different stages of your life, and they will all impact you for the better, whether that be them making your life easier or teaching you a lesson. It is better not to be stuck in the past, but to learn from the experiences. Sure, it's normal to dwell, but don't linger there for so long that you forget to live!

When I reminisce about the direction of my life and play the time machine game, I remember the story of how the late great Chadwick Boseman struggled with cancer for four years. His life was coming to its demise, with only limited people knowing. He could have chosen not to pursue his career in his final days, but instead, he continued to thrive and persevere.

We must remember that we can live a life of abundance, and that great things shall prosper. The past is the beginning of our storyline. The present creates our path. The future is still unwritten, but is influenced by what you learn from both of the others.

You need the mental forward motion to process and progress. To elaborate, this means to find the root cause of why you are the way you are, figure out how you can change, and commit to working each and every day to live in your purpose.

Take it one step at a time. Rome was not built in a day, so don't expect your journey to manifest as quickly as you may have planned.

GUIDED QUESTIONS:

1. *Name a time in your life that you would travel back to if you could.*

____

____

____

____

____

2. *How would your life be different if you made different decisions?*

____

____

____

____

3. *Who are the people in your life that make you feel blessed to have?*

____

____

____

____

Inspiration Sources:

- *The One Thing* by Gary Keller
- *The Secret to Success* by Eric Thomas

CHAPTER 4

Stop Screwing Yourself Over With Entitled Thinking

*"Develop and grow that muscle to be with the uncertain in life.
To be with the glory of life itself,
unconstrained by your own limits and opinions."*

— *Gary John Bishop*

We must look internally to see why our minds play games and tricks on us. When will we learn that life is what we make of it? When will we begin to see the difference between the parts of our lives that work for us and the parts that only hinder us?

Acknowledging that you could be the problem preventing you from being great is highly important as you build your mental muscle. There comes a point when we have to identify that we are screwing ourselves over. We aren't only hindering our growth, but holding our blessings and talents hostage through self-doubt.

Screwing yourself over revolves around three components: limited beliefs, self-sabotage, and entitled thinking. These components can lead you to move in the wrong direction, a route with no focus on the importance of your mission in life. Acknowledging these components shall help guide you to prosper in what you feel is successful, rather than what society tells you is successful.

Limited Beliefs

Limited beliefs come from fear, not understanding the unknown, and comfort zone thinking. This can occur when you dwell on what society tells you about who you are and who you are destined to become. We all know that it is easy to stay in our comfort zone.

Still, this gets you nowhere. It only results in us not accomplishing the things we desire to do in life. You will continuously hold yourself back when you allow these limited beliefs to govern you.

You can explore until you discover what is unknown. Everyone has what it takes to be great inside of them already. We will either take action or continue to think about taking action and get stuck there.

Your limited beliefs can come from your upbringing, societal expectancies, the environment you are working in, among others. Yet, we all have the power to change. But if you don't possess the mentality to continuously show up for yourself, how can you change?

There comes a point in your life when you have to learn what you are willing and unwilling to put up with. Maybe you had a bad upbringing, have been in toxic relationships, or you're struggling with a dead-end job. It's still on you to make changes for the better. We all have what it takes to get out of our head; stop thinking in terms of limitations, and begin to think in abundance.

Self-Sabotage

I first heard the concept of self-sabotage through a podcast called *G-code* by local radio personality AdriVi. She discussed having self-doubt within herself on the career decisions she was making. She identified this way of thinking as the one thing that could have hindered her from the success that she has accomplished. Self-sabotage is vitally important to acknowledge as you're working on your path to what you feel is success.

As the second component of screwing yourself over, self-sabotage happens when you purposefully set yourself up for failure. You let those inner thoughts get the best of you. You allow how people think of you and judge you to stop yourself from unleashing the greatness within. You hold back from reaching your full potential, and, most of all, going after your destiny.

For inspiration, you can look at the people you feel are successful. Who do you consider to be the "greats?" Do you not think that Daymond John had doubts and fears while creating FUBU? Have you ever considered that P. Diddy had points of time when he was scared that his music label Bad Boy Records was going to fail? Do you believe that Oprah was not worried when she moved from her TV show to her *own* network station?

Every person with a success story had moments and thoughts that could have sabotaged them. But, they stayed consistent. They built mindsets that would allow them to prevail and seek success. This determination is part of how they became known today.

Self-sabotage is normal, but we can't let that hinder us from shooting for excellence and going after what we desire. It's going to be a bumpy road, but if you want to be better you will have to go out and get better. At the end of the day, you are your biggest critic, and the only person that will ultimately stop you from being great is *you*.

Entitled Thinking

Now, what in the world does entitlement have to do with screwing yourself over? According to the Merriam Webster Dictionary, entitlement is "the belief that one is deserving of or entitled to certain privileges."

When you are entitled, you have the disposition that you are supposed to be given what you feel is rightfully yours, when that is not always the case. Of course, it would be ideal to be treated a certain way with a prestigious reputation, but that isn't always the case.

In life, there are those who are given things, and there are those who earn what is rightfully theirs. We describe the rich as having silver spoons in their mouths, and they often develop entitled thinking through how they were raised. On the other hand, those that earn the things they want will have a sense of humility and appreciation for the hard work that got them to their destination.

It depends on you putting yourself out there to get exposure to make your life how you want it to be. For example, one of the most hated players in the world is Lebron James. He worked hard to get where he is today, but he could have had an entitled mindset about his championship and reputation.

Of course, do you think LeBron James believed he was entitled to earn a championship? Maybe Lebron believed he was worthy and had the skills to get multiple titles. Still, he had to work hard just like the greats were before and after him to get that title.

He also had to develop great leadership skills by getting his teammates involved, working on his game on the court, and staying out of scandals off the court. He remains humble because he utilizes his talents and gifts for the greater good, and he has never forgotten the kid from Akron who wanted (and continues) to give back to his hometown.

The way to stop screwing yourself over is getting a handle on your limited beliefs and start taking action in exploring new opportunities. There are opportunities all over the world.

It's on you to make changes that are necessary to get to the next level in your life.

Self-sabotage comes with negative thoughts that are holding you back from not realizing the greatness inside of you. You have to take 100% ownership of your life. Nobody owes you anything. You want the life you envision, so go for it and make it happen.

You need to have a laser focus on the things that will make your dreams reality. It's all about building momentum, which will require that mental muscle to overcome the unforeseeable, the impossible, and the uncontrollable. In life, nothing goes exactly as planned, and when you understand that, you can prosper.

GUIDED QUESTIONS:

1. *What limited beliefs do you have, and what can you do to counteract them?*

____

____

____

____

____

2. *How has self-sabotage hindered your growth?*

____

____

____

____

____

3. *Do you have an entitled mindset? If so, how can you change that?*

____

____

____

____

Inspiration Sources:

- *UnF*ck yourself: Get Out of Your Head and into Your Life* by Gary John Bishop
- *The G-code* Podcast by Adriana "AdriVi" Viverette

CHAPTER 5

Turning Losses into Lessons

"Keep working. Keep striving. Never give up.
Fall down seven times; Get up eight."

– Denzel Washington

This is one of my favorite quotes because it makes me think of all the losses (aka Ls) that I have experienced in life! They have manifested as failed familial relationships, failed romantic relationships, missed career opportunities, and many other setbacks.

A fellow entrepreneur and friend shared this wisdom with me once, and it has stuck with me for years: "A setback is a setup for a major comeback."

In *Becoming,* the documentary about Michelle Obama, she was asked about falling off after a situation! Her response was that picking yourself up is not about getting back on track, but starting out on a new one.

To me, Michelle is the epitome of what it is to have a life that looks perfect from the outside. However, she made a big change when she decided to walk away from her career to be the first lady. She made sacrifices to go around the country and rediscover herself by supporting her husband's political career and reinventing who she was as a woman.

Sylvester Stallone Before Rocky

Yes, I'm a big *Rocky* fan, but the history behind the storyline is the important part. Let's talk about the movie's writer, Sylvester Stallone. Stallone first wrote the *Rocky* script in the mid-1970s. It took him twenty hours in a timeframe of three days to complete the script.

Stallone went through some trials and tribulations in the beginning; nobody wanted to buy his script. It got so bad that he sold his dog Butkus (the real dog in the movies) for fifty dollars because he couldn't afford to take care of him anymore.

When a director finally showed interest in purchasing his script, they wanted to have a real Hollywood star. But Stallone persevered, and he was adamant that he would be the main actor for the movie. He was offered $360,000 with the condition that he didn't play Rocky, but he turned it down.

Stallone was also going through personal struggles at home with a baby on the way, a struggling marriage, unpaid bills, and only $106 in the bank. But he didn't let the mishaps of his life hold him back from what he believed. Eventually, Stallone sold the script for a fraction of the initial offer, and he got to play Rocky.

He purchased his dog back and the movie's success led to him winning three Oscar Academy Awards, including Best Picture, and the movie grossed over $200 million. The release of his movie led to a franchise with over $1.4 billion in revenue. By rolling with the punches, just as Rocky did in his fight with Apollo Creed, Stallone's passion and determination to stick to his dreams throughout life's hardships allowed the *Rocky* franchise to be one of most successful movie franchises of all time.

The Legendary Michael Jordan's Challenges

During his sophomore year in high school, Michael Jordan was cut by his high school basketball coach. His coach felt he wasn't developed enough to be on the varsity team. This challenge could have led Michael Jordan to be an unknown and unrealized legend. But Michael believed in himself.

He practiced day and night to get onto the team. He trained faithfully to grab the attention of the coach in the fall season. Michael proved his worth to his coach and was eventually scouted by colleges all over the country. Today, he is a Hall of Famer with six NBA championships.

Michael could have taken the criticism of the coach to heart and given up on his dream, but he had faith that his talent was extraordinary and he was destined for greatness. He built within himself the mindset that he could overcome, and he is true testament to the fact that developing that mental muscle takes grit, resilience, and determination to conquer anything that comes your way.

The common moral of these success stories is that failure is part of life, but if you know how to pivot that failure into a learning experience, you will be a step closer to being the person you are destined to be. Stick with your values and don't back down when the going gets tough. **Keep going**. See things through and watch how the hard work manifests into something great.

GUIDED QUESTIONS:

1. *What losses in your life can you now say were lessons?*

____

____

____

____

____

2. *What is preventing you from overcoming your failures to move forward in life?*

____

____

____

____

3. *Think of a story (celebrity or personal) that resonates with you and reflects the idea of turning losses into lessons.*

____

____

____

____

Inspiration Sources:

- *Becoming* by Michelle Obama (Netflix)
- "Fall Down Seven Times; Get up Eight" by Denzel Washington (YouTube)

CHAPTER 6

Be the Overcomer, Not the Victim

*"A victim mindset is a choice. Since you can choose to see yourself as a victim or a professional a** whooper, which would you prefer?"*

— Finding Love after Heartbreak, Vol 1.
By Stephan Labossiere

It is easy to point the finger at somebody else and blame them for the bad things that happen to you. However, there comes a time when you need to stop wanting to be the victim and start being the victor. No matter what you are going through, I'm a firm believer that God puts challenges in your life because He knows you are capable of handling and growing from them.

I'm a true example of being consistently knocked down while trying to make my way to the top. I went from going to college and then during my final years after walking the stage finding out I failed my final class as well as missing credits to getting my degree.

Then I had taken three years off from school to take a break from completing my degree because I was lost in life and didn't have confidence in myself or the unworthiness of being a college graduate. When I finally returned, I want to not only get my bachelor's, but also my master's. After accomplishing this, I finally got my dream job, only to get laid off soon after and never returning to the engineering field.

I could have let the lost seven years of accomplishing my bachelor's degree put me into a state of playing the shoulda, woulda, coulda game, but the burning desire that was in me would not allow it. I concluded that engineering was a part of my journey but not my mission, and that was okay.

Engineering gave me skills that I can utilize in other perimeters of my life. For example, when I was in my engineering classes, it would sometimes take us twenty to forty-five minutes to complete one problem. Some tests only had three problems, and we had two hours to complete them. These engineering problems were difficult to say the least, but they equipped me with better problem solving skills and more patience, which benefits me to this day.

I could have played the victim role. I am, after all, a failed engineer. But, I now know that engineering wasn't my calling. Although I still love math and science, I knew I had chosen the field for the potential salary more than anything else, certainly not for a sense of purpose or fulfillment. I overcame the misstep and misunderstanding of my calling, and in turn, learned something about myself: I was meant to serve others.

This inspirational breakthrough and desire to serve others has led me to realize that I want to help other people turn their lives around so they can become whatever their hearts desire.

Dwayne "The Rock" Johnson

Everybody knows The Rock either from WWE wrestling, or as a high-profile professional actor, but that isn't how his story started. He started as a full-scholarship football player for the Miami Hurricanes. He won a championship title, and his aspirations were to go pro in the NFL. He did get drafted, but due to many injuries, he ended up getting replaced.

Johnson could have given up his lofty ambitions, but he chose to keep going. He still tried to pursue the field of football, but later turned his interest to wrestling, where he earned his well-known nickname, "The Rock." Once he had reached his goals in wrestling, he again changed gears and set his sights on a new career as a well-known actor.

Dwayne Johnson could have been a victim, but, even in times of adversity, The Rock was cooking up bigger and better dreams. He put in the work to ensure that one failure would not decide his true potential in life.

He is the definition of an overcomer, and I hope that his story inspires you to not let one setback keep you from reaching for your even most far-fetched dreams.

To give you more examples of those overcomers that made inspirational breakthroughs, here are a few that inspired me:

- **Inky Johnson** lost his dream to go pro due to injury and is now a well-known professional speaker.
- **Bethany Hamilton,** the *Soul Surfer* girl, has a movie about her story. Her arm was bit off by a shark, but she still went on and continued surfing.
- **Eric LeGrand Rutgers,** defensive tackle, was paralyzed during a play and lost his dreams to be pro. Still, he went on to be speaker and philanthropist on behalf of Christopher Reeve (Superman) Foundation,
- **Vinny " the Pazmanian Devil" Pazienza** made a comeback as a boxer after a spinal injury where most believe he would never play the game he loved again.
- **Oprah Winfrey** went from being a victim of rape to a billionaire owning her own TV network.

There are definitely thousands, if not millions of stories, but these are just some of my most memorable and impactful ones. So, maybe your first dream didn't happen. You can still be the victor by overcoming what life throws at you. Ed Mylett said it best, "Things didn't happen *to* you, but *for* you."

Instead of looking back at your challenges and thinking, *why me*, learn to see the value in the lesson and think, *thank God it was me*.

Your story is still being written. Some stories end early; some are never told, and some are ready and waiting to be unleashed. I recently heard another entrepreneur say that this life is ninety percent mental, and I am here to tell you we all have the tenacity to shoot for excellence with the correct mindset that you **can** and **will** reach your goals. The choice is up to you; continue to live as a victim or learn to be the overcomer!

Now that you have dealt with the building blocks and foundation for success, it's time to build your mindset into a winning attitude and mental fitness that will allow you to overcome anything that comes your way.

GUIDED QUESTIONS:

1. *Name somebody you are inspired by how they started as a victim and overcame that situation to utilize their circumstances for the common good.*

2. *Why do you think it is important to think overcoming is a rewarding feeling of winning at life?*

3. *What action steps are you going to take to get out of the victim mentality, and what is your resolution to be the overcomer that you are?*

____

____

____

____

____

4. *What is an inspirational story that displays where a person could have remained a victim but unleashed into a victor by overcoming their situation?*

____

____

____

____

____

Inspiration Sources:

- *Finding Love after Heartbreak, Vol.1* by Stephan "Stephan Speaks" Labroisse
- *Max Out Your Life* by Ed Mylett

CHAPTER 7

Build the Mental Muscle

"Unconsciously, through our good habits, we are creating a good life, good financial health, good physical health, good mental health, and overall feeling happiness."

— Tom Corley in Change Your Life, Change Your Habits

You might be wondering what I mean when I refer to building your mental muscle. Let's first define the two words individually. The Webster Dictionary defines mental as "relating to the mind, its activity, or its products as an object of study," and muscle as "to make one's way by brute strength or by force."

If you combine the two, you can define mental muscle as being in relation to the mental activity to build uncommon strength by force. So, therefore, with time and experience, you will acquire a mindset of wisdom to replenish or grow; the choice is yours.

Building your mental muscle takes time! Surgeons don't get where they are with the snap of their fingers. A body builder doesn't build their physique with no routine workout regimen. An NBA champion doesn't win without practicing consistently and helping their team work together toward alignment with a winning culture. Each of these examples support the fact that building up mental muscle will require discipline over a period of time.

Nas said it best, "I know I can, I know can be what I wanna be if I work hard at it."

I'm here to tell you to go after your dreams, to strive for greatness, and to work on your mission. You will have to acquire the momentum to build a mental muscle that will lead to great opportunities, and good or bad experiences you can learn from. I believe there are two components involved in this: developing good *habits* and a strong *burning desire.*

Habits

Learn to create better habits that will get you to the path you envision to be on in life. It takes time to build a habit, as the cosmetic surgeon Dr. Maxwell Maltz wrote in his self-help book, *Psycho Cybernatics: A New Way to Get More Living Out of Life*. In this book, Dr. Maltz explains that it takes twenty days to create a habit and ninety days to make it a permanent part of your lifestyle.

It will take a master of technique and repetition to prosper into greatness. The habits you create are learned from those that you consider successful, and you should emulate their process and make it into your own unique routine.

For instance, the founder of Amazon, Jeff Bezos, worked twelve hours a day for seven days a week shipping books and products early on in his life. The owner of the Dallas Mavericks, Mark Cuban, didn't go on a single vacation for seven years while he was building his first business. There were times when he stayed up until two in the morning to get work done and eventually become a billionaire.

The William sisters, Venus and Serena were up at 6:00 am at the age of seven and eight years old leading to them winning twenty-eight grand slam championships between them.

So, what do these stories mean?

These self-made billionaires built great habits that steered them to success over a long period of time to get to where they are now. Their mental muscles were built with the constant repetition of routine with grit and willpower in their daily activities.

These habits were reflected in their performance, and they were able to not only accomplish their goals, but far exceed their own imaginations. They were in the mindset to strive for excellence as they worked on building their mental muscle.

Burning Desire

"Excellence is an art won by training and habituation. We do not act rightly because we have virtue or excellence, but we rather have those because we have acted rightly. We are what we repeatedly do. Excellence, then, is not an act but a habit." – Aristotle

These habits will develop through the burning desire for more. And, make no mistake, it has to be a *burning* desire for you to make the needed transition to do more in this life. The mind will play tricks on you and give self-doubt, impostor syndrome, and negative thoughts, but it's on you to decipher the truth.

You are worthy of great things; your breakthrough is coming, and the hard work will pay off. We all go through things, but sticking with it will be so rewarding.

Eric Thomas states that "the only thing you need to get your breakthrough is a strong desire. It starts with you, and it can start as soon as you are ready for it to start."

To be the best you have to emulate and learn from the best! It's a process that you can conquer if you continue to move forward. Building the mental muscle comes with having a routine, building high performance habits, and being around the correct people to get to the next level.

No excuses; just continue to grind, work, and progress forward! Transformation is key to impact and making a difference. That starts with building the momentum to build a strong mental muscle.

GUIDED QUESTIONS:

1. *Name three to five things you need to do to build a winning mentality.*

____

____

____

____

____

2. *What are some burning desires you have?*

____

____

____

____

____

3. *Name three habits you want to build and three habits you want to discard.*

____

____

____

____

Inspiration Sources:

- *Change Your Habits, Change Your Life* by Tom Corley
- *Psycho Cybernatics: A New Way to Get More living out of life* by Maxwell Maltz
- *High Performance Habits* by Brendon Burchard

CHAPTER 8

Weird Over Average

"Comfort makes more prisoners than all the jails combined."

– Grant Cardone

I have never tried to fit in. For as long as I can remember, even back in my high school years, I didn't consider myself a jock, a geek, or a part of the popular crew. But I was definitely known by many.

I learned at an early age it's okay to be weird. In fact, being weird is better than fitting in. It's okay to do things differently and get laughed at because it comes with the territory of building a stronger mindset.

The stronger the mindset is developed from what you feel success is, the company that you keep and making the success into a reality. It comes with great sacrifice to be original and extraordinary, because not everybody is meant to understand your vision. Grant Cardone (aka Uncle G) discusses the concept of omnipresence in his book *The 10x Rule*.

Omnipresence is defined as "the state of being present in places at all times." Omnipresence and being original correlates with getting your message out there to the community that you will impact. I understood this when I attended the 2019 10X Growth Conference. The most memorable thing Cardone stated at the conference was, "if the people don't know you, they don't follow you."

If you believe in yourself enough to walk into your mission of greatness, you have to be willing to put yourself out there fully knowing that you may face rejection and criticism. The people that are intrigued by your weirdness, and who can relate to you, will follow you. It's all about continuously staying weird by doing what you feel is best over being average.

Rick Warren stated, "Insecure people are always worrying about how they appear to others. They fear exposure of their weaknesses and hide beneath layers of protective pride and pretensions."

Looking back now, after reviewing my high school years, I can remember the people who wore all black or sported extravagant hair colors, and I commend and admire their bravery. They were discovering themselves and being comfortable in their own skin. It takes a lot of courage to learn to love yourself, and that comes with creating wisdom and confidence through life experiences.

Being comfortable within oneself is a mental muscle that is developed and can take years to acquire. Listed below are a few great examples of how some celebrities persevered in going after their dreams regardless of the adversities. They took that leap of faith in attracting the people that would understand their vision, and they went all out because they believed in themselves.

- Steve Harvey was a comedian laughed at by many, but is now respected by millions.
- Tyler Perry went from sleeping in his car, to going after his dreams in the film industry, and is now a billionaire with his own studio.
- Steve Jobs started Apple in his garage, and it has grown to be one of the most prominent hardware and software companies in the world.
- Noah built an ark while the town was laughing at him, but he did what he was assigned to do, and has one of the most memorable stories in the Bible.
- Sam Walton went from working on his family farm to building one of the world's largest retail corporations in Walmart and Sam's Club.
- Oprah Winfrey went from dealing with childhood poverty and domestic violence to becoming the first African American multi-billionaire.
- Grant Cardone was addicted to drugs, and then became a sales guru developing the multi-millionaire 10x empire with a one-billion-dollar real estate portfolio.
- Daymond John went from working at Olive Garden to now being the CEO of FUBU and an established businessman known as an investor/TV personality on *Shark Tank*.
- Viola Davis survived childhood poverty to being the first African American woman to achieve the "triple crown

of acting" with an Academy Award, an Emmy, and two Tony Awards.

- Tiffany Haddish was living in her car while pursuing her dream to be a comedian. Now, she is one of the most popular loved comedians and actresses today.
- Eric Thomas transitioned from being homeless and a high school dropout to a number one motivational speaker with a doctorate in leadership.
- FedEx founder Frederick Smith started as a student at Yale University writing a term paper on outlining overnight delivery. His professor gave him an average grade. Yet, now he is a multinational delivery service-company.
- McDonald's founder Ray Kroc was a creative and outside box thinker salesman. He used this to create a multi-billionaire fast food chain (mind you, he never flipped a burger in his life).

All of these examples support the fact that developing the mental muscle to handle adversities is the way to achieving greatness. You can accomplish anything you put your mind to, so I challenge you to go out, be a little weirder, and see where it takes you.

The only thing you have to lose is being average.

GUIDED QUESTIONS:

1. *Think of a celebrity or person you admire who has inspired you by overcoming adversities, and now has an extraordinary story.*

2. *Why does their story inspire you?*

3. *What things might be weird to others but you think are extraordinary?*

Inspiration Sources:

- *Be Obsessed Or Be Average* by Grant Cardone
- *The Purpose Driven Life* by Rick Warren

CHAPTER 9

Make it Happen; No Excuses

"When you want to succeed as bad as you want to breathe, then you will be successful."

— Eric Thomas

We all have the potential to grow and succeed. But, we all have to individually define what success means to us. Some think in materialistic terms and see success in possessions like gold chains, designer clothes, and extravagant cars, but these will ultimately be unfulfilling. Others believe a great job or business, a respectable family, or a nice house are the signs that they've made it. It's all about the choices you make, and the actions necessary to progress forward toward your idea of success.

To acquire a winner's mentality, you need to take action on going after your dreams, turn nothing into something, not limiting yourself with what you don't have, and most of all, get assistance to get the results you desire to have.

The difference between the greats and all the others is that they don't back down on their dreams, but continue to push forward. Yes, as you get older your dreams will evolve, and so should your mindset. I can tell you with certainty that you will not have the same mindset as an adult that you had when you were a teenager. Wisdom comes from learning what you can tolerate in your endeavor in order to move forward in improving your life. As mentioned in Chapter 4, you can choose to stay stuck or get over yourself and make things happen.

How does this relate to building a mental muscle? Well, it comes from the four degrees of action by Grant Cardone; "You can either do nothing, retreat, take normal levels of action, or take massive action." Yes, it can be scary to take the necessary steps to make a life of happiness, joy, and fulfillment, but if you are just going with the flow and take limited steps, how do you expect to prosper?

Eric Thomas said, "If you quit, no day will be your day." So, I suggest you go for your dreams. You can hold yourself back by not making things happen, or you can take action and see the things that manifest. Mindset comes through motion, and muscle comes from momentum built over a period of time based on putting the work in.

GUIDED QUESTIONS:

1. *What excuses do you consistently make for why your life is not prospering?*

____

____

____

____

____

2. *List five things you want to change in your life within the next one to two years.*

____

____

____

____

3. *What action steps are you willing to take to make these changes into reality?*

____

____

____

____

Inspiration Sources:

- *The Secret to Success* by Eric Thomas
- *The 10x Rule* by Grant Cardone

CHAPTER 10

Be Intentional

"There is a part of your brain that filters in information that is most important to you called the Reticular Activating System. The people that are successful in life are the ones who have been able to train their RAS to be obsessed about what they want."

— *Ed Mylett*

In life, as you continue to grow, you will either develop a mindset to dwell on the past or to continue to elevate the wisdom you have gained over the course of your life. Being intentional is about taking action on what you say you are going to do.

Yes, you must be mindful of the present, but that doesn't mean that you can't go on with making the most of your life. We all have choices that dictate whether we will thrive or simply survive in life.

The mind works in mysterious ways, and we have to be *conscious* of what we *subconsciously* learn about that may be magnetically consuming our time. It is okay that you are not where you want to be, but it's never too late to develop stepping stones based on a plan of action.

Don't overthink it. I teach my clients and mentees about my method called P.E.M. This is **p**lanning, **e**xecuting and **m**onitoring what is necessary to get that idea out of your head and into motion. We can all do great things exceedingly and abundantly, but many will never know your story if you don't turn your dreams into reality and tell the story of how you got there.

In his book, *Stop Doing that Sh*t*, Gary John Bishop states, "Luck is for those who cannot define their success, and if you cannot clearly define it, you will most likely never be able to repeat it."

To me, this means that while you are being intentional about going after your dreams and goals, it is not by luck that you will be successful. You get to that place in life by having the mindset to go forward and execute the task. It's about pivoting what is now and into what *can* happen with consistency.

Consistency can be difficult to manage . But in time building a mental muscle, you will endure what routines are best to become the best version of yourself. I ain't gonna lie to you, there are going to be days where you are not going to feel like doing anything, but I assure the hard work of consistency will pay off.

You have to keep the faith through consistency. The sacrifices you endured to accomplish your goals will prevail into the person you were destined to become. You have to have faith over being fearful because this will make or break what you will accomplish and where you get in life. The work ethic you put forth will determine the outcome. There will be times when you think of raising the white flag, but this just means you are close to your breakthrough.

I have had those moments in my life where I was so close to accomplishing my goal, and then I would second-guess myself. This was me self-sabotaging what I was destined to be. Although I didn't successfully make it into the engineering field, I can say that the experience of finishing what I started taught me perseverance and tenacity.

I was intentional, and I didn't give up when the going got tough. Sure, I took some time off, but my resiliency to complete my degree never wavered. I learned that I can do anything I put my mind and time into with a corrective plan of action and a consistent work ethic.

During the writing of this book, I was intentional about the fact that I wasn't going to go another year simply *saying* that I wanted to write my own book and become an author. I went out and did the work, and now this book is coming into fruition.

Regardless of how much time it took to write my book, or how many early mornings I had to spend writing before going to my nine-to-whenever job, I made the commitment to write every day and meet consistently with my publisher. This is the kind of mental shift it takes to be more intentional. For over five years I kept saying I was going to write my own book, and now I have accomplished it.

I am mindful of the year we have had as we get through the pandemic, but we should continue to be intentional in going after our dreams and accomplish the goals we have been yearning over for years. What are you willing to sacrifice to go for your dreams? Are you going to focus on the potential of your future or dwell on the things you can't change?

As I said in Chapter 3, you can't live your life in the shoulda, coulda, woulda. Your mindset will shift as you get older, and it will either elevate you to prosperity with wisdom, or hinder you. The choice has always been up to you!

The Taraji P. Henson Story

Speaking of choices, I would like to talk about the Taraji P. Henson story. If you haven't already noticed, I love writing about celebrities and their beginning journeys. There are lessons to be learned from the beginning stages of these success stories, and how they went from a life of struggle to a groundbreaking moment that changed everything for them. Taraji P. Henson's life story is so intriguing to me, and it's a great example of being intentional and mindful of one's current situation.

She was twenty-six years old when she left home to move to L.A. She took her infant son with her and had $700 to her name. She was leaving an abusive relationship to go after her dream of being an actress. She made a promise to herself and her son to never give up. Taraji was inspired to go the distance and reach for the stars, and she became a prestigious well-known actress.

Recently, she was inducted into the Hollywood Walk of Fame and received her star in 2019. Taraji was intentional about shooting for excellence, never giving up, and leading by example for her son. She was mindful of finding the strength within even when the naysayers thought she was too old to make it, but she is still prevailing at the age of fifty.

Taraji said, "Every day you wake up you have a choice for today. You either choose fear or you choose faith."

So, remember to be intentional in everything you do, because you only have one life to live.

One life to make a change.

One life to make a difference.

One life to pursue a mission with meaning and purpose.

One life to really go for it, because what do you really have to lose?

GUIDED QUESTIONS:

1. *Name five core values that you can be intentional about to find success in life.*

2. *What gifts or talents do you have that can impact others?*

3. *What things do you need to stop doing that are sabotaging your life?*

Inspiration Sources:

- *Max Out Your Life* by Ed Mylett
- *Stop Doing that SH*T: End Self-Sabotage and Demand Your Life Back* by Gary John Bishop

CHAPTER 11

Life is What You Make of It

"Be thankful for what you have; you'll end up having more. If you concentrate on what you don't have, you will never, ever have enough."

— Oprah Winfrey

We can all say, at one point or another in our lives, that we are not where we wanted to be. As I mentioned previously, we hold ourselves back through self-sabotage, entitled thinking, and limiting beliefs. We can retreat and do nothing, or we can take action.

It's time to take ownership that you are not where you want to be in life because of *you*. I'm not surprised that you had setbacks. Honey, that is life. What you do from here on out to move forward is on you.

All of the people I have spoken about within this world didn't dwell on what they didn't have; they used their gifts and talents to go for it, and when they failed they got back up. I looked up to them, and their stories set the tone of what it means to climb their way up from the bottom.

Some were homeless, going after their dreams while living in their car, and endured rejection after rejection until their breakthrough finally happened.

I always say to myself as a mini motto, "Remember how you started and that will keep on going!"

Life is truly what you make of it.

Zero to Millionaire

A lot of self-made millionaires rise from their pain and utilize it for the impact they make. Throughout all of her shortcomings and family dysfunctions, Oprah increased in abundance and built an empire that continues to evolve.

There are many self-made millionaires out there who decided to shoot for greatness despite being told it was impossible. They built their mental muscles to excel with grit, determination, and the acceptance that failures are learning experiences.

Your mindset will be crucial in your journey to success. Your mindset will determine how long you live, how much money is in your bank account, and how many opportunities come your way. Just as we all have the same twenty-four hours each day, we all have ability to become self and people-made millionaires

Silver Spoons (Making It and Not Making It)

Let's take a moment to talk about those who are born fortunate. This book is not meant to bash or downplay the accomplishments of anyone who was born into money.

What I have learned from watching people like this is that money and trust funds don't always guarantee that a person will be able to level up and do more. For example, it is rare for professional basketball players, football players, and even the children of musicians to make an impact in their league or industry because they may take their resources for granted.

Some were destined to do other things which are not in line with their family legacy, and they are unsure what to do in life because they don't know how to make their own impact.

I am not going to go into the specifics of which celebrities or heirs didn't make it because that's not what this book is about. I don't want to downplay their personal struggles or shame how they raised their children. The point is that we all can make it, regardless of upbringing or life circumstances. We all have the ability to strive for greatness.

Striving for Greatness is BS if...

We all have the ability to strive for greatness. But it's BS saying it and not taking action. Yes, we can verbally say I am striving for greatness whether it's one time a day or hundred times a day. But if you are not taking action in executing daily, how are you supposed to see the transformation of where you started to where you are going? This is why life is what *you* make of it.

Life is what you make of it by:

- How you wake up every day.
- The habits you create.
- The lessons you learn from changing losses into experiences.
- How you are accomplishing goals to be the best you can be.
- How you study others to how you study yourself.
- How you network with people to stay stagnant or to be with people that align with your growth.
- How you take action to level up or level down.
- How you overcome becoming a victim of a situation to how you became a victor.

We all have the ability to be great and strive for greatness but life is what you make of it.

You want to start that business? *Do it.* You need to get away from people that don't align with your mission in life, cut them off or love them from a distance. You want to go pro in basketball, football, tennis or swim?

As Nike says, "Just do it!"

Your story is still being written but you only have one life to live, *so stop wasting it.* Keep going and elevating. Celebrate the small wins, but continue to prosper and be the best you.

It doesn't matter who you idolize, you should know more about yourself over anybody else. That is a whole topic in probably another book.

Right now, as a reader, build that mental muscle. If you do, you can make anything happen no matter what obstacles come your way because you are worthy.

You just have to be willing to do the work and continue to learn from those who are already succeeding to implement what you can do in your life to be the best version of yourself. Know this, your life story will be created based on choices and decisions you make.

Recently, I read *9 to 5 Millionaire* by Jemal King. In it, he wrote, "If your dreams feel like they're being delayed, maybe you're the one that's not ready for the dream. There's a process between dreaming and making a dream come true."

It's normal to be scared but it's worth wasting more time delaying the inevitable. Stuff is going to happen. How committed are you to your dreams and to the future?

The next chapter will go further on your past, your present, and your future (which is still being written).

GUIDED QUESTIONS:

1. *Are you thriving or surviving in life?*

2. *If you are thriving, what can you do to make things even better?*

3. *If you are surviving, what changes do you need to implement to make a difference in your life and the lives of others?*

Inspiration Sources:

- *Jump* by Steve Harvey
- *9 to 5 millionaire: Don't Quit Your Day Job* by Jemal King

CHAPTER 12

Your Past Doesn't Dictate Your Future

"I wasn't defined by my past, but I was refined by it."

— Kim Gagné

As you are going forward in life, you have to identify the mental triggers holding you back from developing solutions to push forward. In *Sister Act 2*, I was inspired by the teachers and students to overcome self-doubt, conquer self-sabotage, and not to be discouraged over not being where I want to be in life.

You know, it's really inspiring how you can implement this movie's mini-messages and subliminal moments in your life to this day. I challenge you to view the books you read and the movies or TV shows you watch with an intentional attitude. Look deeper within the message being told, and think about how you can implement it into your life.

As your future is still being written, the messages that

intrigue you can help evolve into the person you envision yourself to be. For example, I heard a speech by motivational speaker and hip hop preacher Eric Thomas (aka ET). He talked about how many people know the stats and points of professional sports players, or they know the entire storyline of a favorite TV show, but know nothing about the stats and storyline of their own life.

I found his speech moving because it illustrates how the past can stay with us if we don't deal with the things holding us back. As I get older, I am learning that life often feels like a TV series with ongoing seasons.

There is an old saying that people are in your life for a reason, a season, or a lifetime. This is part of learning that our lives will continue to develop from the past to the present. The future is always being written, and is based on the decisions and occurrences that will come along in your life.

You must live and think for the future, while staying mindful of what is going on in the present and understanding that the past can hinder or strengthen you.

I heard a memorable quote on one of my all-time favorite TV shows, *This Is Us*: "It's the tragedies that define our lives. They are the fence posts on which the rest of our lives hang."

The way we handle tragedies and life crises will show our true nature and resilience. Critiquing what you have done right or wrong along the way will establish how you handle new challenges in the future.

On the radio, Steve Harvey recently mentioned that Bishop T.D Jakes gave him the advice that "you can't drive your car looking at the rear view mirror." This advice is wise, because although we need the rearview mirror to back up and be aware of our surroundings, we also need to keep our eyes focused forward so we can move to our next destination.

You can look back at the past and learn from it, but keeping your eyes focused on the road ahead gives you the ability to see opportunities for prosperity. Prosperity will come with learning to have faith in yourself.

Your life is a journey and you must manifest what you want to believe, achieve, and receive in this lifetime. The next chapter will discuss how to develop your mental muscle by utilizing manifestation and forecasting based on your work ethic and determination.

GUIDED QUESTIONS:

1. *Create an execution board with your life plan that outlines the action steps you will need to make to meet your goals.*

____

____

____

____

____

2. *Name a time in your life when you developed the required mental muscle to overcome something.*

____

____

____

____

3. *What are the things you want to manifest by developing your mental muscle?*

____

____

____

____

Inspiration Sources:

- *Visionistas: Women Who Think outside The Box — Volume 1*
- *Sister Act 2*
- *This Is Us*

CHAPTER 13

Believe it, Receive it, Achieve it

"If my mind can conceive it,
and my heart can believe it,
then I can achieve it."

— Muhammad Ali

Life has a certain mystery to it that can be good or bad depending on how you look at. It can be bad if you tend to look at life with fear and misery rather than optimism and positivity.

This reminds me of a recent change in my life from transitioning out of a rooming house to an upgraded three-bedroom. Some may ask me why I stayed in the rooming house for five years. Well, I can honestly say I had to regroup my life and shift my mindset from limited beliefs to self-assurance.

Yes, I had plenty of time to move out, but I had to go through a healing process after coming out of a nine-year toxic relationship. I had to rediscover who I was and understand my self-worth as well as the greatness within me.

It took time for me to process a new way of thinking to heal from the relationships that were no longer in existence. I developed new habits that would evolve me such as going through the 75 hard challenge back in 2019 to strengthen my mental toughness in life. Then I figured out how I can still utilize the skill sets from my degrees which can still impact others in this world.

The moral of my story is that you can win in life by having grit, perseverance, and the tenacity to overcome anything that comes your way. It is also important to enjoy the journey and have fun working toward your dream. While building perseverance and the ability to overcome, remember the word *gratification*. Gratification can either be instant or long term. As a society, we are so used to instant gratification that we struggle to wait and work for the things that take time to happen.

We want them to happen immediately, but it doesn't always work that way. I remember hearing the analogy of slow cooking beef stew or chill. This can be illustrated with the analogy of a microwave and a crock pot. The microwave might give you food that is ready to eat quickly, but a meal that has been carefully monitored and slow-cooked in a crock pot will always be more nutritious and delicious.

Beef stew being microwaved rather than being cooked in a crockpot makes the food taste way different. In the same way, you should always lean toward taking the long term approach toward any goal that you may be working toward. The fastest and easiest route is not always the best route.

In her book, *How to Become a Conscious Creator,* Ana Kevelyin Reyes states, "Your thoughts are the building blocks to your physical life, so, choose wisely." You must be conscious that if you believe in receiving your dreams, then you can achieve making it a reality. A strong mental muscle will help you create a vision that can be incorporated into what is coming up the pipeline of your life.

The Lion Story: Jason Weaver

A good example of staying true to one's beliefs is the story of Jason Weaver, the voice of Simba in the *Lion King*. Disney offered him two million dollars up front to work on the film when he was a teenager, but his mother was wise. She declined the offer and renegotiated that he would have a salary of $100,000 up front along with a share of the royalties, which to date has accumulated to over $2 million.

Jason Weaver and his mother believed that it would be a mistake to take the instant gratification of a massive payout, knowing that Jason would miss out on lots of revenue for years to come. By resisting the temptation, they achieved the long term goal of being profitable for generations to come.

In time, and with practice, your mindset will learn to perceive the difference between the easy (instant) or hard (long term) route to your goals. Distinguishing these and making the correct choice will determine whether you are going to win in life.

In the final chapter of this book, I will discuss how to activate your winner's mindset, and offer mental hacks and tips on sustaining that mental muscle.

GUIDED QUESTIONS:

1. *What are you grateful for?*

2. *What are the core values you would like to stay true to throughout your life journey?*

3. *What mindset practices do you need to acquire to sustain a strong mental muscle when life hits you with the unexpected?*

Inspiration Sources:

- *Everyone Needs a Hero* by Sir Aime Zing
- *How to Be a Conscious Creator* by Ana Kevelin Reyes

CHAPTER 14

It's Time to Activate Your Winner's Mindset

"If you want to change your life,
change the quality of questions you ask yourself each day."

—Tony Robbins

Reaching your maximum potential in life takes grit, perseverance, focus, determination, and a mental muscle that has the ability to win ethically but at all costs. We all are put on this Earth to work on our purpose, but very few will seek and truly go after our loftier goals.

We can stay in survival mode, or we can thrive to excellence. Greatness is upon you, but it's all about knowing the right questions to ask yourself each day. I recently finished reading *Traffic Secrets* by Russell Brunson, and every day he asks himself, "How can I give myself a raise today?"

At the time of reading this book, I have to give a big shoutout to my hometown, Buffalo Bills. We have come so far by getting into the playoffs back to back years, and win or lose, I can see how the momentum of their progress as a team will create a winning culture for years to come.

For over three years now, they have built toward this winning culture by learning to prevail while consistently being considered the underdog. Being the underdog has its advantages, because many people will not anticipate your next move, and that's a powerful component to have when you are playing to win.

No matter where you stand in life, you have the choice to win or lose. You have the ability to go after your dreams or let them slip away. You may believe your calling is one thing right now, but your life may be destined for more.

Here are a few examples of people who are still winning, regardless of whether their lives turned out the way they thought they would.

- Ed Mylett had to give up his dream of being a professional baseball player, but he is still winning today as a nine-figure earner.
- Inky Johnson gave up his dream of being a professional football player, but he is still winning and credited as a well-known motivational speaker.
- Eric LeGrand became paralyzed from the neck down, forcing him to give up his professional football aspirations, but he continues to work on finding treatments and doing charitable work as a speaker.

Many of the other greats that I have mentioned in this book have stories just like these. They turned their setbacks into major comebacks, and they are winning at life!

To wrap up, I want you to think about this equation:

Pain + Passion + Purpose = Mission Work

Your **pain** is something you need to acknowledge. Learn how to not let it hinder you. By utilizing your mistakes as lessons, and not letting it stop you from growing and developing your mindset and mental muscle, you can unleash that fire inside of you. That fire will ignite the **passion** to do something that is bigger than you!

I say all the time, "My mission is bigger than me," and that comes from moving with **purpose**. The purpose of your life should stay firm with your values, and should be aligned with what works best for you and God's will for you. Your **mission work** is the daily effort you put into each and every day to do what God has assigned you to do!

I want you to remember these winner mindset tips:

- Trust the process; enjoy the journey.
- It takes a village to build someone up while they are shooting for greatness.
- Stay true to your morals.
- Serve first rather than take.
- Give more than you receive.
- Learn to heal from past pain.

- Be intentional about which direction your choices are taking you.
- Don't perceive failure as limitations, but as opportunities to soar.

Lastly, I would like you to remember two mantras I created and I live by:

- Remember where you started and that will keep you going.
- If you want better, go out, and get better.

Now that you have the tools and resources to have a winner's mindset, continue to strengthen your mental muscle. Shoot for the stars and don't quit going after dreams. Be intentional on being weird or average; the choice is yours. Don't give up in life cause greatness is upon you. So, go activate your mental muscles *now*! You got this!

With the conclusion of this book, please answer your final responses to send me your responses from the guided questions to my IG (@shayonamission).

GUIDED QUESTIONS:

1. *What does mental muscle mean to you?*

2. *Who do you need to add or subtract from your life to have a strong winning circle?*

3. *Rate your current mindset on a scale of one to ten. If ten is the ultimate winning mindset, where do you fall on that scale? If you aren't a ten today, what can you do to get there?*

Inspiration Sources:

- Tony Robbins How to Change (YouTube)
- *Major Payne*

Acknowledgments

First, I would like to acknowledge God for pouring into my heart and using me as his vessel to the mission of writing this book to serve others. I would also like to thank my friends, family, and all of those who have impacted my life. I had so many points in my life when I wanted to give up. I am so happy that God put you in my life, whether you were in my life for a reason, a season, or a lifetime.

Thank you to everyone who helped me build my **MENTAL MUSCLE**, because without you, I would not be the person I am today.

Made in the USA
Columbia, SC
23 March 2025